MAXIMILIAN,

AND OTHER POEMS:

BY

JOHN CHARLES EARLE, B.A.,

AUTHOR OF "ENGLISH PREMIERS," ETC.

In aid of St. Vincent's Home for Destitute Boys.

London:
BURNS, OATES, & Co., 17 & 18, PORTMAN STREET, AND 63, PATERNOSTER ROW.
SOLD BY ALL BOOKSELLERS, AND AT ST. VINCENT'S HOME,
NORTH END, FULHAM.
1868.

In the interest of creating a more extensive selection of rare historical book reprints, we have chosen to reproduce this title even though it may possibly have occasional imperfections such as missing and blurred pages, missing text, poor pictures, markings, dark backgrounds and other reproduction issues beyond our control. Because this work is culturally important, we have made it available as a part of our commitment to protecting, preserving and promoting the world's literature. Thank you for your understanding.

CONTENTS.

	PAGE.
The Death of Maximilian	5
Pulchrina	7
Cardinal Colomba	9
Onward and Upward	11
The Baron's Leprosy	12
The Foundling	14
The Dervishe of Khorassan	15
Bring me Coral	16
Sacred Ambition	17
The Dove's Nest	18
The Tuneful Spring	19
The Sultan's Diary	20
Time not Short	22
Come once again	23
"Not all a Dream"	25
Pan	28
Pope Gregory III.	29
Milton	31
Conscience	32
Epaminondas	34
One is best	36

Seven of the following pieces have already appeared in print, and one of them, "Pulchrina," has been recited in a public lecture.

[COPYRIGHT RESERVED.]

The Death of Maximilian.

IF I had listened while thy voice had power still to save,
   If I had followed thee, my wife, across the eastern wave,
   If I had left a barbarous race to reap the seeds they sow,
I should not wait to-morrow's morn, their shots to lay me low.

There is a freshness in that fount, a fragrance from those limes,
And musical at evenfall break forth the convent chimes;
But, ah! the peaceful cloister now is made the haunt and lair
Of beings treacherous as snakes, and fiercer than the bear.

I will not wreak my wrath on them: the altar there inspires
Far other thoughts than vengeful ones, far holier desires;
For through the canopy of leaves and tendrils I can see
The symbol of my only Hope—the Man Who died for me.

And thy dear face, my youthful bride—I wear it next my heart,
The last remains I have of thee, from which I ne'er shall part.
Oh, face that I have loved so well, oh, gentle—shattered—brain,
When shall our severed lives unite, when, when be one again?

How little, in those golden days when first I made thee mine
And linked the House of Hapsburg with thy father's royal line,
How little could I then foresee the destiny in store –
The rebel's fate succeed the crown which Montezuma wore!

The slave sold in the market-place is rich compared with me,
Of all the Aztecs held I leave not one bequest to thee—
Not one but this light lock of hair, which to my lips I press
And steep in these fast-falling tears of manly tenderness.

Yes, manly, for I will not let the ruffians bind my eyes:
I mean to look on Death, nor shall he take me by surprise.
I mean to bare my bosom to Juarez' murderous fire;
I mean to fall as Kings should fall, and as I lived expire.

Forgive them all, O GOD, nor let this land for me be curst;
Forgive the wretch that sold his lord—of all my foes the worst:
Forgive them as I too forgive and hope to be forgiven—
The victim of disunion here seeks unity in Heaven.

Now as he spake it came to pass; and at the dawn of day
The Emperor, shriven, knelt at Mass, then calmly led the way,
And to the Generals with him doomed, in accents nowise sad,
Said, " Come now, Gentlemen, *vamos nos a la liberdad!* "

The friars came with cross in hand, and groups of Indians bore
Three coffins up the mournful steep, the lancers rode before;
The heavy death-bell tolled the while a funeral march was played;
And where three sable crosses crown'd the height the cortége stayed.

The Emperor marked the rising sun; he clasp'd in warm embrace
His Generals* and the Bishop, then he gazed on Charlotte's face,
And with her miniature in hand—his arms cross'd on his breast—
He gave the sign, and, pierced with balls, he entered into rest.

---

* Miramon, and the faithful Indian, Mejia.

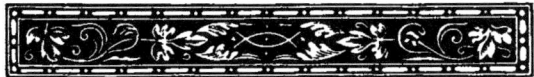

Pulchrina.

HEN the Church was in her cradle, rocked by Persecution's storm,
Signs and judgments sent in mercy kept the faith of Christians warm;

Hearts of unbelief were cloven by the Spirit's sudden fire,
And the heathen, wroth with idols, trod them piecemeal in the mire.

Beauteous as the moon when rising, or snow mountain tinged with rose,
Stood Pulchrina, maid of Gnatia, pure as any star that glows,

Meekly waiting for the moment when her torturers would try
All their fiendish arts to make her GOD the only True deny.

Golden-tressèd was Pulchrina, and her hair dishevelled fell,
Like a mantle wove of sunbeams, o'er her figure moulded well.

Never yet in any region failed such loveliness to sway
Human breasts, however barbarous, and incline to pity's way.

Therefore with a mien less Gentile, and in milder suasive tone,
To Pulchrina, maid of Gnatia, spake the Prefect from his throne—

" Though the Emperor's mandate binds me thus to judge thy lawless crime,
Fain my clemency would spare thee;—break thy stubborn will in time.

" For one act of recognition of the immortal gods of Rome,
Still thy father's arms shall clasp thee, and conduct thee scathless home.

" Mark the effulgent godhead yonder of Apollo, lord of day;
Point but to his genial disk, then free and joyful go thy way."

Then Pulchrina, blest confessor, pointed downward to the dust;
" Cursed be all they," she cried, " who in such idols place their trust.

"What are suns, and stars, and systems? He who made them can destroy;
He whom only I adore can crush them like an infant's toy."

Foamed with rage the Roman Prefect—"Hasten, bind four horses wild;
Goad and lash them till they tear her limb from limb, presumptuous child!"

Bound, and lashed, and goaded were they, but the coursers would not stir,
Stood as still as if at pasture, tightening not one cord on her.

"Lo, the minx hath practised magic!" to his slaves the Prefect cried,
"Loose the coursers; yoke yourselves; and of a score the strength be tried.

"Forty hands her impious carcass limb from limb will tear with ease.
What! the craven wretches falter!—drag not!—fall upon their knees!'

Even so: they all were kneeling (posture of man's utmost might),
And a crowd of Gnatians marvelled at the strange and solemn sight,

While a score of voices clearly rose to heaven and humbly prayed—
"GOD of gods, the GOD of Christians, loose Pulchrina, righteous maid!"

Beckoning to the eagled helmets, "Soldiers," roared the Prefect, "strike!
Spear them in the name of Cæsar, sorceress and slaves alike!

"Let their flowing life-blood's savour the insulted gods appease;
And let every Nazarene take warning by the fate of these."

Scarce the dire command was issued, when the frenzied Prefect fell
Headlong from his seat of judgment, struck by hand invisible;

For a flood of fever rushing swiftly through his murderous brain,
Whelmed him in a fatal vortex, and he never spoke again.

Then Pulchrina, maid of Gnatia, free and joyful hastened home;
And the people vowed her GOD was greater than the gods of Rome;

And the twenty slaves, converted, ere the morrow's dawning ray,
In the Church's quickening laver washed their Pagan sins away.

Cardinal Colomba.

Pope Gregory X. presided at the Fourteenth Œcumenical Council, held at Lyons in 1274. A temporary union of the East and West was there effected, and the Oriental prelates accepted the formula "Who proceedeth from the FATHER and the SON."

AZING toward the Alpine regions on a couch at droop of day,
On a balcony of marble Cardinal Colomba lay.

"*Eminenza*,"* said his nieces, "wherefore on the vacant sky,
In the midst of pangs so dreadful, fixest thou that piercing eye?"

And he answered, "I am waiting for the downy-breasted dove,
Through the depths of glowing ether, mission'd on a task of love."

Then they thought he spake in figure, like a prophet or a seer,
When his words to wondering listeners fill their joyful breasts with fear.

"Well we know there needs no waiting for *His* advent," they replied;
"Long th' Eternal Dove has settled in thy heart and at thy side.

"Long His sweet inhabitation, shining even through thy face,
Makes thee altogether dove-like—Dove by name and dove by grace."

"Lo!" he said, "reflected sunbeams kindle all her breast to gold,
While before her winnowing plumelets cloven clouds a path unfold.

"Lo! by strongest instinct guided, hither slopes the carrier dove,
Through the depths of glowing ether, mission'd on her task of love.

---

* An anachronism. The epithet was not applied to Cardinals till a later period.

"When the holy Pontiff parted Gaulward, to the council bent,
And upon the long-sought union of the East and West intent,

"Thus he promised: 'I will send thee, for thy prayers' and sorrows' sake,
Back, if all succeeds divinely, this same carrier dove I take.

"This shall be the happy token that our vows are heard, if thou
On the tiny scroll of vellum find καὶ παρὰ τοῦ υἱοῦ.'"*

While he spake the winged courier o'er the garden poised awhile,
Recognised her favourite dove-cote 'neath the villa's warm slate tile,

And toward the marble terrace dropping, with a parchment tied
To a golden-threaded necklace, rested at Colomba's side.

Stroked he then her silken plumage, stroked her bosom, neck, and brow,
And, with palpitating rapture, read καὶ παρὰ τοῦ υἱοῦ.

And the vision of the council seemed upon his gaze to burst,
And he heard the fathers chanting in sonorous Latin first,

Then in Greek, the sacred symbol of the faith decreed at Nice,
With the *Filioque* added as the final bond of peace.

Soon his overflowing spirit gushed in copious streams of speech,
And beyond her wonted compass seemed with nascent powers to reach—

"HOLY GHOST! the bond of union, from the FATHER and the SON,
Now and evermore proceeding, with them equal, with them one.

"Keep Thy holy Church united, one in every age and clime;
Let the schism foul of Photius perish to the end of time.

"*Nunc dimittis servum tuum;* wherefore should I wish to live?
Life has given me more than ever I had hoped that life would give.

"Far beyond this glowing ether sits another council vast
Of the venerable sages, saints, and patriarchs of the past:

---

* And from the SON.

" Deepest mysteries of matter, mind, and soul, to them more clear
Shine, than shine to us the lessons taught us in our earliest year:

" To their keen and new perception comes, in every sight and sound,
Knowledge turn'd at once to wisdom from Creation's utmost round:

" All our Latin jubilation, thither wafted, mounts and meets
All the psalmody of th' Orient echoing through the golden streets;

" While, in grander tones and sweeter, bursting from that concourse blest,
Psalms of joy attest the union of the severed East and West!"

Here his bitter pangs, recurring, overpowered him, and he died
On the balcony of marble, with the gentle dove beside;

And in marble monumental, chiselled at his own command,
Rested with a dove in glossy agate perched upon his hand.

Onward and Upward.

 PASS the vale. I breast the steep.
  I bear the cross: the cross bears me.
  Light leads me on to light. I weep
 For joy at what I hope to see
When, scaled at last the arduous height,
 For every painful step I trod,
I traverse worlds on worlds of light,
 And pierce some deeper depth of GOD.

The Baron's Leprosy.

"PILGRIM from the holy places, welcome to our ingleside!
Crackling fagots feed the blazes; share our cheer, 'tis Christmastide.
Lay thy staff and wallet by thee, and thy hat with scallop shell,
And some tale of thine adventures to us, eager listeners, tell."

Then he spake—the wayworn Palmer, seated in the ingleside,
'Neath the berried boughs of holly, in the mirthful Christmastide,
In the spacious hall baronial, while, without, the northern blast
Through the forest sere was howling, and the snow was falling fast.

"I was in the golden city where the LORD of glory died,
On the very slope of Calvary, where my GOD was crucified,
Kneeling 'neath the lamps suspended day and night above His tomb,
When a warrior stood beside me, half in lustre, half in gloom.

"'Palmer,' quoth the knight in armour, forward bent, in accents low,
'Erst a stalwart chieftain was I, now a leper white as snow:
Lest my envious rivals learn it, lest our foes should gird my fame,
Underneath this mail and visor I conceal my loathsome shame.

"'Noblest Norman arms are blazoned on my banner and my shield,
And five hundred horsemen follow when I scour the battle-field:
Syrian hordes like chaff they scatter; never from their lines they swerve:
Will their valour work such marvels now my arm hath lost its nerve?

"'Moslems I have hewn in pieces with too much of human rage;
'Gainst them more than 'gainst my passions hitherto I warfare wage.
Pray the GOD of health to heal me, for He hears when pilgrims cry;
Ask His mother blest to aid me: thou art holier than I.'

"Pity seized me while he shivered, and I heard the jostling links
Of his shaken corslet and his head-piece clanking at the chinks;
And with forehead on the pavement, at our dear Redeemer's tomb,
'Great Physician,' prayed I, 'heal him: save him from the leper's doom!'

"'Lo,' he said, 'I feel thy prayer hath power against the foul disease:
Cold and clammy sweats bedewed me; now they pass; I move at ease.
Fast subsides the prurient tetter, and to-morrow's morn I dare
Hope to sit at Godfrey's* council, hale as any champion there.

"'Take, O man of God, this grateful offering; take this purse of gold.'
'Heaven forbid,' I answered firmly, 'that my prayers be bought and sold.
Give thy bounty to the poor, and glory unto Him whose grace
Causes prayer and prayer's effect:' and, saying thus, I fled the place."

Then a murmur of applause ran through the old baronial hall,
And the lord of Noron, rising, stood and spake before them all:
"Now thrice welcome to my castle! I have sought thee far and near
Through long caravans of pilgrims: Heaven hath led thy footsteps here.

"It was I who stood beside thee at our dear Redeemer's tomb,
Cased in steel, the abject leper, half in lustre, half in gloom.
Hark! without, the sturdy branches swinging, crashing in the blast;
But the furious storm is powerless here within my fortress fast:

"Be my home thy bourn of peace. Here let thy toilsome travel end:
'Twas thy puissant prayer that healed me; I will be thy lasting friend.
At the lord of Noron's table sit henceforth an honoured guest,
And among my faithful people in thy last long slumber rest."

---

* Godfrey of Bouillon was chosen King of Jerusalem in 1099.

The Foundling.

DOWN in a dell of diamonds, that glittered in noonday,
Beside a pool of sapphire, a new-born infant lay:
Her flesh and form were delicate; the blood which in them glowed
In currents noble of descent or gentle must have flow'd.

"Oh, ruthless mother," I exclaimed, "what evil hast thou done!
Why hast thou in the desert left thy lovely little one?
'Twere better far to bear thy shame upon thy nursing breast,
Than have the conscious heart within by heavier load oppress'd.

"These drops of diamond dew all blood will sparkle in thine eyes,
And thou wilt seem to hear thy babe uplift her feeble cries,
And thou wilt shriek in dreams to see ferocious beasts and wild
Out of these rosy brambles spring to fasten on thy child."

I seized a she-goat GOD had sent a-browsing alongside,
And scooped a gourd to fill with milk in bubbling spirts supplied,
And near the baby in my lap the rude green cup I placed,
And of the dulcet draught I coaxed her tender lips to taste.

But when her failing force revived, I plucked some plane-tree leaves,
And laid them o'er her unswathed limbs, more innocent than Eve's;
And in my mantle's fold I brought the tiny foundling home:
"What is a burden now," I said, "a treasure may become."

Well, eighteen summer suns have shone upon the lively shoot,
Which in my heart, as in my house, has stricken deep its root;
And Time, who brings so much to light, denies us any clue
To her whose deep-dyed hands deposed our darling in the dew.

And never have I ceased to bless the day when, in the wild,
I found upon a violet bank my own adopted child.
She's passing fair, and good as fair; she's all in all to me;
And, if you'll stay ten minutes more, you'll see her—make the tea!

The Derbishe of Khorassan.

ONE midnight I sank on my pillow, exhausted with pleasure and wine,
  With pleasure that long had been loathsome, with wine that could not make me glad.
 I slept; and a Vision before me said, "Go, when the morning shall shine,
And prove in the place I will show thee how sweet a thing 'tis to be sad.

 "Beneath a tree far in the desert, the corpse thou wilt see of a saint :—
  His water-skin, staff, and torn garment, be thine to the end of thy days."
 I found them ; and, doffing my gay clothes, I lost every breath of complaint,
  And took up thenceforward for ever to Allah this burden of praise :—

 "There was nothing in me more than others why Thou shouldest choose me in love ;
  There was nothing in me more than others, save that I exceeded in sin.
 Thy choice is not founded in merit; Thy grace like the light from above,
  Has nought in the darkness it conquers, but scope for its lustre to win.

 Withhold from me all that thou willest, my will shall be ever with Thine ;
  In penury, pain, and abasement, my fate is Thy bondsman to be ;
 Estrange Thyself from me by coldness, that coldness shall never be mine,
  Thou seekest from me no advantage, how dare I be selfish towards Thee?"

 Three things I ask daily of Allah, that ne'er among men I may be
  In honour, nor have for the morrow provision of water or crust,
 And, chiefly, that when I am dying, His face I in mercy may see :
  Two prayers have been fully accorded, the third He will grant me, I trust.

 We are not two separate spirits; though mine is encompassed with clay,
  It lives but in Allah, and only in oneness with Him can be blest.
 It is not through fear that I serve Him ; it is not from hope any way;
  I love Him because He is lovely, and take small account of the rest.

 Adorable will of my Maker—how little it leaves me to ask.
  My doctrine, my bliss, and my duty, may all be summed up in a word;
 To repeat it myself and to others is more than enough for life's task,
  For nothing more sacred than ISLAM* on earth or in heaven is heard.

---

* "Submission to God." The language used in the above lines may be found in the sayings of Dhou-el-Noun, Fodheil, Halladj, and many other Mahometan ascetics. Its near approach to the writings of Saints and Fathers of the Church is obvious.

Bring me Coral.

BRING me coral, bring me shells,
    Nautilus or glittering sand;
    If it in the great sea dwells,
If it loiters on the strand
If it tosses on the brine,
Bring it me, and make it mine!

Bring me pearls, or bring sea-weeds
    From the gardens of the deep,
From the green and watery meads
    Where the long-locked Nereids sleep,
Bring me jewels from the caves
Chambering the drowsy waves

Whatsoever Thetis hides
    In her beating bosom bring,
Whatsoever lavish tides
    On the agate pebbles fling;
All things silvered by the sea
Have a token-charm for me.

Ah! my straining eyes, how oft
    To the more alluring sea
Turn they from the clover croft
    And the scantly herbaged lea,
Watching every sail afar
Where my heart's two treasures are.

Never have I loved but two—
　　Never shall I love a third ;
One is buried in the blue,
　　And, whene'er the wave is stirred
Into music, every billow
Lullabies my love's last pillow.

Never have I loved but two—
　　Never shall I love a third ;
One is blown about the blue,
　　Every windy whistle heard
Wafts my loved for evermore
Where I wait him on the shore.

Sacred Ambition.

AST thou indeed
　　Sacred ambition,
In word and deed
　　Based on contrition ?
Pray low and long,
　　Sowing and weeping :
Promises strong
　　Pledge thee thy reaping.

Thus hast thou pray'd ?
　　Wait then contented :
Blessings delay'd
　　Are blessings augmented.
Everything proves
　　Holy ambition
Is what GOD loves
　　Next to contrition.

The Dove's Nest.

SAW a dove from roof to roof
  And rock to rock a crevice seek,
  And turn, with tender plaints, aloof
Her creamy bosom soft and sleek.

At last the lone and weary bird
  An odorous almond-tree espied,
The liquid ether gently stirr'd,
  And straight into its centre hied.

And under eaves of leaf and spray
  And showering tufts of blossoms fair,
She found a chink, and 'gan to lay
  Her couch of down, and nestled there.

O pleasant dove, O favoured tree
  That harboured such a guileless guest!
I would my love were like the dove,
  And I the almond-tree, her nest.

And soon a brood of dovelets play'd
  Around the hollow on the lea,
And tried their callow strength, and made
  A dovecote of the almond-tree.

O pleasant dove, O favoured tree
  That harboured such a fruitful guest!
I would my love were like the dove,
  And I the almond-tree, her nest.

The Tuneful Spring.

YPE of poets, tuneful spring,
    Gurgling near the apple trees,
Where the tall stakes in a ring
    Overladen branches ease,
Prop the ruddy fruit, and form
Apple bowers in orchards warm;

Carol softly for my sake;
    To my music-loving ear
Cadence after cadence wake
    In the more than mellow year;
In the tempered autumn-tide
Sing and babble, shoot and glide.

Murmur sweetly, while, around,
    Juicy fruit, in every breeze,
Tumbles on the thymy ground
    Of the maizy hempen leas,
And the ephemeral dragon-fly,
Warm'd to new life, arrows by.

Purl beside the poplar roots,
    Serenade the sleepy wood,
Irrigate the garden fruits,
    Bubble 'neath the village rood,
'Long the ivied abbey wall
Seek thy rest or waterfall.

I should love to be like thee
    On thy water-cresséd ways,
Pure and constant in my glee,
    Clear and flowing in my lays
Fed from sources deep and strong,
And my very being song.

The Sultan's Diary.

THE Sultan, they say, is a bit of a wag,
And laughs in his sleeve to hear Englishmen brag
Of the marvellous progress of civilisation
Where so many mendicants die of starvation.

In his journal just published in Turkish we read—
"It seems to be part of the Englishman's creed
To raise at the corner of every street
A palace for gin, and for drinking it ' neat.'

" They talk very much of the worship of God,
And being so pious, it seems rather odd
They multiply shrines to the honour of Bacchus,
And, though we are temperate, still they attack us.

"If you walk out at night, as I often have done,
With a hat, not a fez, for a good bit of fun,
You will see on all sides how they hiccup and stutter,
And, porpoise-like roll without shame in the gutter.

" Now, Allah be praised, and his prophet, that we
Have only one GOD while these Christians have three;
And we find in the Koran no warrant for thinking
Human beings, like fishes, should always be drinking.

" It was but last year that a million of snobs
(For it takes thereabout to make one of their mobs)
Tore down in Hyde Park every bit of the paling
While Vic., the Lord Mayor, and the council were quailing.

"Let them say of 'the sick man' whatever they please,
I would not rule over such subjects as these—
As easily kindled as matches of phosphorus;
There's far better order maintained in the Bosphorus.

"The women, I swear, are as bad as the men,
And I never did shake so with laughter as when
The Viceroy of Egypt was mobb'd at the Zoo
By ladies, and that on a Sunday eve too!

"How very polite now all this to a stranger!
His coat-tails, you know, were in imminent danger,
And he took to his heels just as if a *copella*
Had slipp'd from its case in pursuit of the fellow.

"It's a fatal mistake to let women run loose;
For my part, I'd hold them in tight with a noose;
In the harem secure, with a veil on the face,
They save you a world of expense and disgrace.

"It really gives people a terrible handle,
And causes a deal of both comment and scandal,
When they frisk so on horseback, and drive in the park,
And ogle the men into love for a lark.

"And that Rotten Row—it may well be called rotten,
If you think of the ills that of it are begotten;
It's at best, as they told me in various quarters,
A pretext for trotting out unmarried daughters.

"Her majesty seems to abuses quite callous,
And is a sham Queen in her Buckingham Palace;
She is no more a sovereign than I am a people;
The state is to her as the church to the steeple.

"The mob and the Commons—they manage the boat;
The Lords only register what t'others vote;
And the Queen—if she dared to say no, Mrs. Vic.
Would soon hear Messrs. Multitude cry, 'Cut your stick!'

"This Parliament rule is of all rules the worst;
And England I hold to be specially cursed;
Manhood suffrage, it seems, soon in female will issue,
And the head and the tail will be all of one tissue.

" This comes of rejecting the system designed
By Allah Himself for the good of mankind,
That the throne by the Caliphs fill'd never should fall,
And I should, in fact, be the Sultan of all."

Abdul Aziz writes thus in his quizzings diurnal;
Many extracts besides we might make from his journal;
But these will suffice, perhaps, to prove from the work
That he looks at us all with the eyes of a Turk.

Time not Short.

"HOW brief my days!" I oft complain,
   But ere the sigh is past,
I answer in an altered strain,
   "My time will ever last."

Why should I fret that life is short,
   And through impatience fall?
If once I reach the inner court
   There will be time for all.

A million years will roll away,
   While life is in its prime,
A million wonders court delay,
   And still there will be time.

Lord, let my guardian angel school
   My steps, severely kind;
And let the march of ages rule
   The motions of my mind.

Come once again.

COME once again. The grapes are glossy here,
   In sunny saccharine savour swelling fast,
   Delays the Tramontana and the blast,
And widow'd wail of the decrepit year.

Yes, come again; and while thy footfall steals
   Beneath the olives with brown berries hung,
   Some canzonet by fair vine-dresser sung
Will charm us, or some holier vesper peals,

Floating at sunfall 'long the purple hills,
   Meet us in some deep valley where the breeze
   Together shakes the scents of shrubs and trees,
And o'er our cheeks the essence cool distils.

The sable gondola with curvéd prow
   Shall wait to ferry thee across the stream
   Where Dian's argent disk with mirror'd beam
Will glitter placid as thy pearly brow.

I love whatever is least like unrest,
   The waters rippleless, the mossy green,
   The bosk unblown, the welkin's cloudless sheen,
The thoughtful brow, the calmly beating breast.

Hiemal rains a gorge have cloven deep;
   There find we seats upon some rocky cube,
   Beside the lance-leaved reed with ringéd tube,
And watch how softly Nature sinks to sleep.

Far overhead the tawny corn shall wave,
 And purpling clusters dangle 'bove the corn,
 And o'er them all the poplar dark upborne
Sustain the star-roof of the blue concave.

We cannot tell how many worlds are ours;
 For all those distant twinkling isles of light,
 Whose glimmer never yet reach'd mortal sight,
Exert on us, no doubt, some latent powers.

Come soon again. The vision of those skies
 Thick-starr'd will foster in us, as it should,
 That mingled sense of our own magnitude
And littleness, wherein true wisdom lies.

Come oft again. By crystal wave, and balm
 Diffusive, mellow fruits, and dewy even
 O'er thoughts inspired will pierce yon golden heaven,
And meditate the everlasting calm.

"Not all a Dream."

ON the shore I fell asleep,
    And I dreamed an angel came
Walking on the liquid deep,
    With his glorious limbs on flame;
All diaphanous and bright
As a topaz in the light.

Something to the sea he said;
    What it was I could not hear;
And I saw a living head
    Straightway on each wave appear,
And like Aphrodite grow
Into beauty's perfect glow.

Then from lip to lip there passed
    Some sweet watchword so intense
In its import, that at last
    In that risen phalanx dense
All the beings bright and strong
Burst into a sea of song.

Ne'er did such a summer sea,
    Vast, melodious, and low,
Of unearthly minstrelsy
    Moderate its ebb and flow,
Ne'er on mortal listener beat
With a pœan half so sweet.

Breathing thus their psalms, the blest
    Gazed entranced upon the skies,
Turning from the darkling West
    Toward an Orient paradise:
And they seemed to see afar
Some stupendous morning star.

Soon the star became a sun;
    And within its disk of gold
Stood th' emblazoned form of One
    Whom the heavens cannot hold,
One in whom all glories shine,
Whether human or divine.

"Hope of Ages," cried the sea,
    "Welcome to Thy bought domain!
Take us where Thou wilt with Thee,
    Or among us here remain!
Like to us is that or this,
For Thy presence is our bliss."

Echoes from adjacent lands,
    Echoes from remotest sky,
From the dead who burst their bands,
    Or descended from on high,
Answered to the choral host
Triumphing from coast to coast.

Then in haloes round their King
    All those holy sons of light,
Ranged in ring succeeding ring,
    Moved in self-sustaining flight,
Bent th' adoring knee in air,
Interchanging praise with prayer.

All the firmament was full
   Of enormous rainbows rife
With those beings beautiful
   Risen to ethereal life;
And th' expanding pageant seemed
Nigh to touch me while I dreamed.

" O my dream!" I dreaming said,
   " For a dream thou surely art,
In the galleries of my head,
   In the caverns of my heart
Linger through the charmèd night,
Linger till the morning light!"

Wert thou but a dream, O dream,
   Or a prophecy of things
Which in after time shall beam
   On the gaze of him who sings—
An assuring far-shot ray
Of the already dawning day?

Pan.

IVER, river, in thy rolling tide
   I behold another current glide;
   Canst thou ever, river, backward flit?
Never, never, river; nor can it.

Forest, forest, through thy area vast
One strange vernal sap is pulsing fast;
In the marvels, forest, of thy green
How much more we see than eye hath seen!

Mountain, mountain, where the azure dome
Rests as on a pillar, mountain home
Of the eagles, morning's beacon fire
Kindled on thee glows with something higher.

What is this, the forest's greener green,
Seen in all things, and yet nowhere seen,
Hard, so hard, so easy to find out,
Source of faith, and end of every doubt?

Awful Spirit! if indeed I be
Worthier than those hills on fire with Thee,
Rushing streams and woods—so much the more
Let me with Thy glorious self run o'er.

Pope Gregory III.

THOU Regal Shepherd, who in fields above
Leadest Thy flocks to founts of blissful life,
Thou who hast made my lowliness supply
Thy place below, and while I led Thy lambs
To pastures pure, hast crowned me also king,
And changed the cross of Peter to a throne,
And murderous masters into subjects mild,
And founded in this great metropolis,
Abandoned by the Orient Emperors,
And by Thy red right arm of vengeance saved
From Leo the Isaurian and his fleet
Whelmed in the Adriatic, whelmed and broken
As he, proud pervert, broke the images
Of Christ and His dear saints,[1]—hast founded here
Such rule as yet the world hath never seen,
A kingdom new and of Thine own device,
A sovereignty especial, and unique,
And sacerdotal, typified of old
By Simon[2] and Hyrcanus,[3] high-priest kings,
Who ruled Thy chosen 'neath the law as I
(Though all unworth such ponderous dignity),
Beneath the Gospel rule this people now:
Mine eyes are dim with clouds of coming death,[4]
Yet something through the gloom I seem to see—
Long lines of splendour on the hills of Rome,

---

[1] A.D. 726. [2] B.C. 146. [3] B.C. 107. [4] A.D. 741.

And thrones successive of her Pontiffs reared
In righteousness, defending throughout earth
The poor, the oppressed, and the Faith assailed.
And, if I list the lyre of prophecy
Aright, the nations far and near will pour
Into the bosom of Thy queenly church
Abundant treasures, and enhance the power
And splendours of this apostolic see.
But if, in days when love is waxing cold,
And many Antichrists the last precede,
And faith is feeble, if the slaves of sin,
Eager for democratic liberty,
O'erwhelm the visible empire of the Popes,
And drive them and their faithful followers down
Into the tear-soak'd catacombs again,
Arise, O Regal Shepherd, in Thy might,
And steep Thy Pontiffs in celestial dews,
And burnish them with such illustrious grace
That, by the sharpest edged conviction pierced,
Their deadliest foes converted may confess
That Clemens, Linus, Peter, live anew!

Milton.

COMBINE me sentiment and soul,
   Invention, grandeur, and profound
   Philosophy, mellifluous sound
And copious image; 'tis the whole

I ask to make a poet crown'd
   Above his fellows, and I find
   Such merits rarely so combined,
On ancient or on modern ground,

As in the sightless bard who sung
   The loss of Paradise, and all
   The thick-veiled mysteries of the fall
Wide open to our fancy flung.

Alas! that gazing on the sun
   Of Justice, that bright eye grew dim,
   Discerned no Deity in Him,[*]
Nor all the Father in the Son.

I hold it better then to be
   A church-taught child in village school,
   Whose faith is measured by her rule,
Than scale Olympian heights with thee,

O Milton, and in doubt descend,
   And standing by my Saviour's cross,
   Turn all its glorious gain to loss,
And in a Deist's portion end.

---

[*] See Lord Macaulay's Essays—"Milton."

Conscience.

"Were it not for this voice, speaking so clearly in my conscience and my heart, I should be an atheist, or a pantheist, or a polytheist, when I looked into the world. I am speaking for myself only; and I am far from denying the real force of the arguments in proof of a God, drawn from the general facts of human society; but these do not warm me nor enlighten me; they do not take away the winter of my desolation, or make the buds unfold, and the leaves grow within me, and my moral being rejoice."—*Newman's Apologia*, p. 377.

SEE the God whom I adore
   In every shell and star,
I hear Him thundering on the shore,
   But see and hear afar.

I see Him in the power of thought,
   The flashes of the ode,
In every nobler precept taught
   By heathen's moral code.

I see Him in the works of taste,
   The engine and the loom,
In Tadmor's ruins in the waste,
   In temple and in tomb.

I see Him in the course events
   Take in this mazy world—
His sunshine upon Israel's tents,
   His foes in darkness furled.

I see Him in His spotless Spouse,
   Her majesty and grace,
In all her symbols, rites, and vows,
   His truth revealed I trace.

I see Him in His children's love,
    Their pure and humble ways:
Whence, if not from the light above
    Proceed such genial rays?

But chiefly in my own calm breast
    I hear, as creeps the day,
His whispered words "Wouldst thou be blest,
    Seek this, and shun that way."

Speak louder, clearer, sacred Voice!
    Till more and more I find
That conscience, which directs my choice,
    Is God within me shrined.

No atheist doubts can ever try
    My faith while thus I hear,
My own existence will supply
    The proof that God is near.

My fellow men, the world so fair,
    The church—all stand around;
His *mark* is on them everywhere,
    But *in* me He is found.

Epaminondas.

THE Theban general falls at last
His hour of long successes past.
With anxious glances on him bent,
His warriors bear him to his tent;
And while the red drops trickle down
His well thew'd limbs, without a frown
Complacently he calls to mind
The glory he must leave behind;
The days he spent at Lysis' feet
And found philosophy so sweet;
The scrolls that made his youthful hours
A summer ramble among flowers;
His fame for letters which had spread
Incipient laurels round his head;
And how from Thebes, the great and free,
The brave Pelopidas and he
Had chased the Lacedemons hated
And on their treachery fulminated;
And how upon the Leuctran plain
The king Cleombrotus was slain
With all his host, and Sparta thence
Fell from her proud pre-eminence,
And Thebes was blest with strange increase
Among the rival States of Greece
And founded Megalopolis.
He thought of those invading ranks
He led along Eurotas' banks;

Of his Thessalian victories;
His grateful country, and the prize
Of new and loftier dignities,
Which for himself he never sought
While for his country's weal he wrought,
Believing virtue's self to be
Sufficient recompense.
     While he
Thus ran in thought through all his life
And through the last and fatal strife
Of Mantinœa, where he gain'd
The wound which now his rough couch stain'd,
He ask'd his Thebans, " Is my shield
Borne safely from the battle-field?"

 Then to the valiant chief replied
His faithful guards, " Thy buckler dyed
In thine own blood is at thy side."
 Epaminondas turn'd again
And kissed his trusty shield, and then
Enquired, " Is victory with our men ?"
  "The field is ours," they all exclaim.
  "The Gods be praised!" he cried, the fame
Of Thebes is still unstain'd, and I
Contented therefore sink and die."

 If when I fall, as fall at last
I must, I can review the past
Complacently, and call to mind
The good name that I leave behind;
If memory brings me records bright
Of patient watch and valiant fight;
Of fields of victory overrun,
Of routed foes and trophies won
In the long warfare against sin
Upon the battle-field within;
Of selfish interests set aside
And for another's weal denied;—

Printed by Libri Plureos GmbH in Hamburg, Germany